SUPERNATURAL

ACCELERATION

HOW I LEARNED A SECOND LANGUAGE IN LESS THAN TWO MONTHS

SUPERNATURAL

ACCELERATION

HOW I LEARNED A SECOND
LANGUAGE IN LESS THAN TWO MONTHS

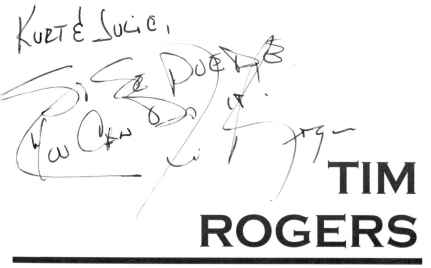

TIM
ROGERS

SUPERNATURAL ACCELERATION
How I Learned a Second Language in Less Than Two Months
By Tim Rogers

Direct quotations from the Bible appear in italic type.

Cover design - Laura-Lee Booth & Jay Hughes
Photography - Josh Adams
Editing & interior design - Laura-Lee Booth

Copyright © 2010 by Tim Rogers Ministries
All rights reserved.

ISBN-10: 1-60683-031-7
ISBN-13: 978-160683-031-4

ACKNOWLEDGMENTS

Nothing of value is ever really attainable in life unless you have a good team helping you. I have been so fortunate to have such a team working with me on this project and would like to acknowledge their participation.

First of all, to my best friend who woke me up at 3 a. m. one morning and told me it was time to write what He had taught me, my Savior and friend, the Lord Jesus Christ.

Secondly, to my amazing wife, Rhonda, who has never ceased to encourage me as I worked on this project.

Thirdly, to three of the most incredible MKs I know anywhere: Hannah, Tiffany, and Matthew. You guys totally rock my world.

Thanks to my mom for being such a prayer warrior. Without your prayers, I might not be doing what I am called to do for the Kingdom.

A special thanks to Aunty Carol for your original edits and for being an eternal encourager. Thanks to Joe Duininck for your amazing input and insight into this project.

Thank you to our incredible staff in Mexico. Without your help, we could not accomplish all that God has called us to do.

Finally, a special thanks to my pastors, Kenneth and Lynette Hagin, who believed in me even when I worked in the mailroom.

IT'S NOT WHAT
YOU KNOW,
BUT WHO YOU
KNOW...

AND WHO YOU
KNOW, COMES
FROM
CONNECTING AND
COMMUNICATING
WITH PEOPLE.

CONTENTS

PREFACE

veryone has a story. Mine is simple, yet remarkably powerful in that it demonstrates what an extraordinary God can do in the life of ordinary people who are willing to obey. It's an amazing story of how God filled a need in my life and accelerated my ministry in a very supernatural way.

I needed to learn another language, but I did not have the time or the resources that were required to do so. Rather than learn a second language the traditional way, I broke the proverbial mold of "common sense" and dared to stretch my faith beyond what I thought was possible. You see, unless you dare to do more than you can possibly do, you'll never be more than you can possibly be.

Having never attended language school, never taken

a Spanish course in high school, and never spoken in a foreign language, I went from knowing only a couple of words in Spanish to standing in a classroom with about 70 students, some notes, and my Spanish Bible in hand, teaching in a Bible school and speaking fluently in Spanish—in only a two-month period of time.

The great news is that God is no respecter of persons. What He did for me, He will do for you. God will give you the ability to reach your own life's goals supernaturally.

◄ ▐▐▐▐▐▐ ■ ▐▐▐▐▐▐ ►

Effective communication is the foundation for any successful ministry or business.

◄ ▐▐▐▐▐▐ ■ ▐▐▐▐▐▐ ►

I will explain the principles that God taught me, which accelerated my ministry beyond what I could have accomplished in this short period of time. These principles, if applied, can be used in whatever area your need may be in. However, in this book, I will only deal with communication—more specifically, learning a second language . . . or even a third.

My purpose for writing this book is two-fold: First, I want to help you connect to others with your God-given gifts. And second, I want to teach you how to move quickly into God's call for your life.

Effective communication is the foundation for any successful ministry or business. Equally so, ineffective communication can be a detriment to any ministry or business.

◄ ▪▪▪▪▪▪▪ ▪ ▪▪▪▪▪▪▪ ►

Learning another language will provide a greater window of expression for your gift.

◄ ▪▪▪▪▪▪▪ ▪ ▪▪▪▪▪▪▪ ►

The challenge of learning another language can be tedious, time-consuming, expensive, and extremely frustrating. A language school can cost thousands of dollars and take months—even years—to complete without offering any guarantee of success. The principles you will learn in this book have saved me years of frustration.

Of course, learning a foreign language did not

come without work, effort, and faith. Yes, that's right. Faith. Believing that *I could*—and *I would*—speak another language. Please don't get me wrong; this is not a "blab it and grab it" message. It's not saying something and— POOF!—like magic, having it. It must be birthed in your heart with conviction, not giving the slightest room for doubt. It's believing with such assurance that you are going to speak in a different language, that when it materializes, you are not shocked.

Knowing another language can open many doors of opportunity in life, including new relationships, new business opportunities, new travel experiences, and a wider range of influence in ministry. Personally, I believe everyone should be bi-lingual, as it gives an even greater expression of your gift and allows God to use you to a maximum capacity.

I challenge you to read this book with an open heart and ask God to impart the same key principles to learning a second language into your life that He imparted to me. As you do so, I believe you will experience the thrill of communicating and connecting to others as you never have before.

REALIZATION OF A DREAM

In January of 1979, I traveled for two months with a team of 60 people from *Youth with a Mission* throughout Mexico. At the time, I was only 18 years old. We went by bus to Chihuahua, Mexico City, Puebla, Vera Cruz, Tampico, and the border town of Matamoros. We slept on the bus, under the bus, in tents, and sometimes in host homes. It was not a five-star luxury vacation by any means, but I loved it! I loved the people, the food, and the country of Mexico with its amazingly rich culture, architecture, history, and beauty.

It was my first real experience in a country where English was not the primary language spoken. I was in one of the most beautiful places in the world; yet I could not fully enjoy it, because I could not communicate with the people beyond a few words and gestures.

If you have ever traveled to a country where the people do not speak your language, you have probably felt the frustration of not being able to communicate properly.

For example, when you're at a restaurant and want to order chicken, you're relegated to pointing at pictures on the menu or playing a game of charades, giving the universal "chicken" sign by sticking your knuckles in your arm pits and flapping your arms—all the while secretly hoping they don't bring you a live chicken! Or, you may have ordered a dish from the menu only to get something quite different than what you thought you had asked for. I'm sure you get the picture!

Later that year, I began classes at RHEMA Bible Training Center[1] in Broken Arrow, Oklahoma. During the school year, I went with a group of 35 fellow students on a week-long trip to Guatemala. It was during that trip that I felt God's leading to return and work with the Spanish-speaking people.

The following year, in June of 1980, I boarded a plane for Quetzaltenango, Guatemala. I had committed to work with a missionary organization for two years, primarily with the indigenous Guatemalans.

Quetzaltenango is a colonial town located in southwestern Guatemala. It is surrounded by mist-covered mountains, one of which was the active Santiaguito volcano. The volcanic activity was so intense that on many days ash would become caked on the cars. I remember many mornings being awakened by tremors so strong that they would shake the pictures off the walls. Despite its volcanoes and tremors, Guatemala is a country rich in tradition and culture.

It became my home away from home, and I loved it!

CHAPTER ONE

KEY PRINCIPLES

1. Language opens the door for opportunity.

2. Decisions determine direction.

3. Don't go until you know.

S.A.L.E.

D uring the two years I worked as a missionary in Guatemala, I did not attend any formal language school. Yet, in approximately two months, I became fluent in Spanish. Although that may not seem possible in the natural, *". . . with God all things are possible,"* (Matthew 19:26b).

I believe God wants to do a quick work in the earth today, and He is accelerating our ability to access knowledge and achieve His goals to touch this world for Christ. What God did in my life was teach me how to have a "supernaturally accelerated learning experience," which I have coined as the acronym "S.A.L.E." Ironically, the Spanish word *sale* means "to go [out]." I didn't realize the parallel meaning until years later. I thought it was pretty cool to know God is always on *GO!*

I had been in Guatemala for only a few weeks when one day, as I was reading the Spanish Bible, it seemed as though scales had fallen off my eyes, and I was able to read the Spanish Bible word for word along with the English Bible. The funny thing was if you gave me a Spanish newspaper, I could not read a word of it. Even today, years later, I find it difficult to read a secular Spanish newspaper, but I prefer to study the Word of God in Spanish.

THE CONCEPT OF S.A.L.E.

In 1980, most of my communication with my parents in Canada was by letters sent through the postal service, which often took months to arrive. Occasionally, my family and I telephoned each other, but that was very expensive. Consequently, most of my communication back then was seldom at best.

Today, however, is a different story!

Communication nowadays has jumped light years since I lived in Guatemala. My daughter is currently attending Oral Roberts University in Tulsa, Oklahoma.

Everyday we can talk free of charge through Skype® or Facebook®. The beauty of Skype® is that we talk through our computers using webcams, so we can see each other while we are talking and it's in real time.

Through S.A.L.E., God showed me how to have a "Skype® communication" mentality, when most people were still using a very slow "postal service" mentality.

The concept of S.A.L.E. is very simple in that God has given us tools for service. These tools are both natural and supernatural, and when put to use and applied, they will produce accelerated results in life.

◄ ▌▌▌▌▌▌▌ ▪ ▌▌▌▌▌▌▌ ►

God...is accelerating our ability to access knowledge...to touch this world for Christ.

◄ ▌▌▌▌▌▌▌ ▪ ▌▌▌▌▌▌▌ ►

The problem is if we only use the natural tools that are available to us, we are not considering the spiritual instruments God has given us to grow and develop. It would be like an emergency room surgeon knowing what is needed for an operation but not having the proper tools at his disposal. Or, perhaps having the proper tools but not having the intuitive instinct on how to operate. Having both supernatural and natural tools creates accelerated progress, and I believe that's how God wants us to live.

CHAPTER TWO

KEY PRINCIPLES

1. Use a combination of natural and supernatural tools, which will produce accelerated results in your life.

2. God desires us to operate in a dual-function mode: We work in the natural like it all depends on us, and we trust in the supernatural like it all depends on Him.

3. God is doing a quick work in the earth today, and He is accelerating our ability to access knowledge and achieve His goals to touch this world for Christ.

MINISTRY BIRTHED FROM DESIRE

For years, I longed to speak another language. I was born in Canada and grew up in a country that had two national languages: English and French. However, like many Canadians who were raised on the West Coast, we rarely spoke French; so I was only fluent in English. Although French is one of our national languages, it is only spoken by 22.7 percent of the Canadian population.[1]

During my first trip to Mexico, a desire to connect with Spanish-speaking people was conceived in my heart. To converse with someone in another language can be quite exhilarating, but my desire went beyond simple communication. I wanted to speak to their hearts in a way that impacted them. I did not want my conversations to be limited to a casual, "Hello, how are you?"

Like many people in ministry, I desired to be able to connect with others, develop relationships and friendships, and impart something into people that would be meaningful. Of all the gifts you will ever receive, the greatest gifts are personal relationships.

Perhaps you have heard the story of the little boy who, in a fit of anger, told his mother he hated her. Fearing his mother would punish him for his harsh words, he ran to a hillside and shouted to the valley below, "I hate you! I hate you! I hate you!" Then, all of a sudden, he heard the echo of his words, "I hate you! I hate you! I hate you!" Running back home, he told his mother there was a mean little boy in the valley saying he hated him. His mother took him back to the hillside and told him to shout, "I love you! I love you! I love you!" The little boy did as she said, but this time he discovered there was a nice little boy saying, "I love you! I love you! I love you!"

Of all the gifts you will ever receive, the greatest will be personal relationships.

What's the point of this story? It's that life is an echo. What you sow, you reap; what you give, you get; and what you impart to others will come back to you. Words are powerful containers. They contain life, encouragement, praise, inspiration, and blessing; or they contain death, discouragement, betrayal, and deception.

This book is about communicating, connecting, and imparting to others by helping them discover their greatness. Ralph Waldo Emerson said, "What lies behind us and what lies before us are tiny matters compared to what lies within us."[2]

As leaders, we must mine the rich deposits of wealth in others, rather than merely giving our wealth to them.

Vince Lombardi, a legendary American football coach, at one time held the esteemed dual position of head coach and general manager of the Green Bay Packers football team, based in Green Bay, Wisconsin. Under his coaching, the Packers never experienced a losing season. In fact, Lombardi is considered by some to be the greatest coach in football history.

A story is told of one hot, humid day when Lombardi's team was having a particularly uneventful practice. Looking over the seemingly unmotivated young players, Coach Lombardi called aside Jerry Kramer, a 250-pound, 6'3" guard. Lombardi, noted for being disciplined and demanding of perfection, had played the same position in college as Kramer now played—not an easy situation for any player. He began to lay it on the line, as only Coach Lombardi could do; telling him that he was not aggressive on the field, not blocking, not tackling, and not putting out! In short, he told him that he was a lousy football player, and that he wanted him to leave the field for the day. The broad-shouldered, strong guard dropped his head and walked off the field in defeat.

◄ ▪▪▪▪▪▪▪▪ ▪ ▪▪▪▪▪▪▪▪ ►

Be a catalyst of good news, a carrier of inspiration and help others discover their greatness.

◄ ▪▪▪▪▪▪▪▪ ▪ ▪▪▪▪▪▪▪▪ ►

Almost an hour later, Lombardi himself left the field and walked into the locker room. Still in uniform, sitting in front of his locker with his head down and shoulders slumped was that guard, quietly sobbing. The coach paused, taking in the scene in front of him. It is said that he walked over to the young player, slipped his arm around his wide shoulders, and spoke to him in a completely different tone. Calling him, "Son," he reaffirmed that everything he had said earlier was true, that he had not seen him play as he knew he could, and that he truly was a lousy football player. But, he then added that he could also see that on the inside of Kramer was an excellent player, and that he intended to stand by him until that excellence came out.

Life is an echo. What you give, you get; and what you impart to others will come back to you.

Jerry Kramer, the young guard, straightened his shoulders and began to see himself in a new light. In fact, he served an 11-year NFL career with the Green Bay Packers and was voted All-Pro five times.

That is the power of imparting to others. Connecting

with someone through a meaningful, heartfelt conversation with the goal of leaving them feeling better
about themselves than when you came.

Bob Harrison is known as America's leading
"Increase Activist." He is a best-selling author and
noted seminar/conference speaker. We have had the
honor of having him speak in our church on several
occasions. Recently, I received an e-mail from Bob
telling me about an article he had read announcing a
rewards program benefiting travelers to and from
Mexico. In his e-mail, Bob said, "The minute that I
read this article, I thought about you. ... I trust all is
well with you and the family. I think of you often and
am so proud of you and all that you are doing."

When I read it, I was so humbled. Here is a man
whose itinerary is full, who travels speaking all over
the world. Yet, when he thought about me and my
family, he took the time to write to us and let us
know that he was proud of us.

That might seem like a simplistic gesture to many;
but to me, it was priceless. Many times, it's words and
thoughts expressed like that which encourage my wife

and I and keep us fired up.

Think about the people who have encouraged you in your life's journey—the times when you were down, depressed, and felt like giving up but someone came along and imparted something to you that kept you going.

We should all strive to be just like this. Let's be a catalyst of good news, a carrier of inspiration and help others discover their greatness.

CHAPTER THREE

KEY PRINCIPLES

1. Of all the gifts you will ever receive, the greatest gifts are personal relationships.

2. What you sow, you reap; what you give, you get; and what you impart to others will come back to you.

3. Be a catalyst of good news, a carrier of inspiration and help others discover their greatness.

LIVING TO GIVE

As ministers of the Gospel, we must examine our motives. We cannot be motivated to accelerate our ministry for selfish gain. The skills and gifts God has given us were given to us for the furtherance of the Gospel. Whether our desire is to learn a new language or any other God-given desire, our hearts must be pure. We cannot desire skills or gifts for wrong reasons.

The "What's in it for me?" attitude is shallow and self-defeating. In the long run, it will not serve the true purpose of learning a new language or any other skill in a supernatural way. Remember, do not use your relationships with people to build your desired skill. Instead, use your desired skill to build relationships with people.

HELP OTHERS FIRST

I love what Zig Ziglar said, "You can have everything in life that you want if you will just help enough other people get what they want."[1] In the book of Psalms, it says this:

> *"Delight yourself in the LORD and he will give you the desires of your heart. Commit your way to the LORD; trust in him and he will do this."*

> **Psalm 37:4, 5 (NIV)**

Learn a new language for what you can give, not for what you can get. This is another key to learning a language supernaturally.

You may be asking yourself, "What do I have to give?" But I think that's the wrong question.

In Acts 2, Peter and John were about to enter the temple when they came across a crippled man begging for money. Peter responded to the man by saying:

"...I do not possess silver and gold, but what I do have I give to you: In the name of Jesus Christ the Nazarene—walk!"

Acts 3:6 (NASB)

The crippled man was totally healed. This miracle opened a door of utterance for Peter to preach his second sermon and 5,000 people were saved! This is a powerful story that provides key insights into fulfilling our God-given dreams. Note that Peter and John *knew* what they had, *gave freely* of what they had, and *were rewarded* with a great opportunity.

◄ ▪▪▪▪▪▪ ▪ ▪▪▪▪▪▪ ►

Learn a new language for what you can give, not for what you can get.

◄ ▪▪▪▪▪▪ ▪ ▪▪▪▪▪▪ ►

Peter and John wanted to bless another human being. They didn't call a prayer meeting and ask five elders to check their profiles to see if they were qualified to help the crippled man. They simply responded from their hearts to help someone in need. And this is how all of us should be.

The question we have to ask ourselves is: "What do I have to give?" Not long ago, I had dinner at the home of Wayne Myers, a missionary friend of mine who has ministered in Mexico for over 60 years. He told me he and his wife, Martha, never let a day go by that they do not give something to someone. In his recent book, *Living Beyond the Possible*, Brother Meyers made this statement:

> *"When you live to bless somebody else, you live in a dimension that is above the ordinary."*[2]

Wow, what a great statement to live by!

Apply that same principle to learning a second language. Determine in your heart to learn Spanish—or a different language—so you can bless somebody else! And realize that when you do, giving first always has a reciprocal effect.

CHAPTER FOUR

KEY PRINCIPLES

1. Do not use your relationship with people to build your desired skill. Instead, use your desired skill to build your relationship with people.

2. Learn a new language for what you can give, not for what you can get.

3. When you live to bless someone else, you live in a dimension that is above the ordinary.

4. Give value first.

THE POWER OF PERSEVERANCE

P eople told me it was going to be extremely difficult to learn a second language as an adult. They said it would be better if I first moved to Costa Rica and attended a specialized language school for a year. But even after doing that, it would take about five years to become fluent in Spanish. I was told a "gringo" like myself could never speak the language like a national. I would always speak Spanish with an American accent. In fact, I was told many things to discourage me from trying.

If there's one thing I've learned over the years, it's that you can never be moved by what other people say or by how long and with what difficulty it took them to learn a different language. A sense of inadequacy comes upon you when you compare your efforts with the success of others. You are you—unique, distinguished, and filled with unlimited potential. God sees things in you that most people don't. More so, He sees things in you that people see but ignore. Remember, perseverance will always outlast persecution.

FORGET THE PAST

One of the major obstacles to fulfilling your God-given dreams is not to understand your potential. The measure of your potential is God's assignment to you, *not* your past mistakes or what others might say about you. Someone said it like this: "Don't judge my future by my past." In Spanish, we say: "No juzgques mi futuro basondote en mi pasado."

RESIST DEFEAT

I love the movie *Apollo 13*. It is based on April 11, 1970—that day in history when a spacecraft bound for the moon became crippled by an explosion when an oxygen tank ruptured. In the movie, Ed Harris played Eugene "Gene" Francis Kranz, a NASA flight director, who was given the bad news by his support crew of the possibility that the spacecraft would not return to earth, he simply replied, "Gentlemen, failure is not an option."[1]

◀ ▐▐▐▐▐▐▐ ■ ▐▐▐▐▐▐▐ ▶

Think about Sir Edmund Hillary. Between 1920 and 1952, seven major expeditions failed to reach the summit of Mount Everest. A Swiss team was forced to turn back only 1,000 feet from the summit.

Perseverance will always outlast persecution.

◀ ▐▐▐▐▐▐▐ ■ ▐▐▐▐▐▐▐ ▶

Hillary knew that many men had died before him and yet his will to succeed was strong. The challenge he faced did not deter his faith from attempting to accomplish something no man had ever done. On May 29, 1953, at 11:30 a.m., Sir Edmund Hillary and Tensing Norgav reached the summit of Mount Everest (29,028 feet above sea level), the highest spot on the earth.[2]

Allow that kind of determination and faith to encourage you to get out of your comfort zone and do more than you possibly thought you could. Learning a new language might not be as difficult as climbing Mount Everest, but once you learn to communicate with others in that new language, you will feel like you have conquered the world!

◄ ▋▋▋▋▋ ■ ▋▋▋▋▋▋ ►

"Failure is not an option."

Eugene "Gene" Kranz
NASA flight director,
Apollo 13

◄ ▋▋▋▋▋ ■ ▋▋▋▋▋▋ ►

Too many people quit the process of learning another language too quickly. It takes patience and fortitude to see the end result. Okay, I know someone might say, "Yeah, that's easy for *you* to say. It only took you two months to start speaking Spanish."

Let me respond by saying that everyone can learn to speak a new language supernaturally and quickly; however, the length of time it will take for *you* to speak fluently may differ from my experience. It will depend on your individual commitment, drive, time, and energy.

Today can be a day of new beginnings, a day of new challenges and rewards. Commit to learn, and enjoy the process. Believe it is working, and you will see results sooner rather than later. Soon, people will say to you, "I can't believe you are speaking so quickly. How did you do it?"

CHAPTER FIVE

KEY PRINCIPLES

1. God sees things in you that most people ignore.

2. The measure of your potential is God's assignment to you, *not* your past mistakes or what others might say about you.

3. Perseverance will always outlast persecution.

4. Be fully persuaded that you will learn a new language, and remember that failure is not an option.

5. Commit to learn and enjoy the process.

THE LANGUAGE OF FAITH

I t takes faith to learn a language. Most of the time, we think of learning as a mental exercise—an intellectual process that requires hours of lectures, study, and memorization. Please don't misunderstand me. There is a process in this learning experience that involves the mind. Actually, it requires a *renewing* of your mind, or a re-thinking process. The mind does have an important part to play.

However, if you want to learn a language supernaturally and quickly, you must apply faith that is not moved by your past, age, lack of education, or what people might say. It starts by believing that *you can* and that *you will*—no "*ifs,*" "*ands,*" or "*buts.*" Faith is being determined, purposed, and committed to the cause. Believe you can, say you can, and don't be moved by feelings.

ACTIVATE YOUR FAITH

One of the greatest things I learned in Bible school was from a man named Kenneth E. Hagin. He taught us about faith and that nothing is impossible to him who believes.

You see, we don't have as much of a "knowing" problem as we do a "believing" problem. Knowledge abounds all around us. If you don't believe me, just Google[®9] "language programs," and you will find over 750,000 responses. However, with all of the knowledge available to us, most people stall out in the believing process. So many people have "how-to" books, CDs, and videos on their bookshelves that teach on every subject from starting a business to becoming a successful CEO, to investing wisely and being free from debt, and to learning how to be a person of greater influence. Yet, with all the information that is available to us, how much of it

> ◄ ▮▮▮▮▮▮ ▪ ▮▮▮▮▮▮ ►
>
> **...we don't have as much a "knowing" problem as we do a "believing" problem.**
>
> ◄ ▮▮▮▮▮▮ ▪ ▮▮▮▮▮▮ ►

do we apply to our lives or become an active part of our thinking processes?

The word *believe* means "to be persuaded of the truth or existence of something." I like to say it like this: to believe is to be fully persuaded of the truth. In Spanish, you would say it this way: *una convicion absoluta*—or in English: *an absolute conviction of the truth.*

To believe in something really has two sides. First, you have to be fully persuaded of the truth; and second, you have to act on that truth if you want to see results. For example, I am fully persuaded—I completely believe—that I love my wife and children. However, acting on that belief through my words and actions is what brings joy, peace, and happiness in our home.

In the same way, when learning a second language, you need to be fully persuaded that you can and that you will succeed.

People don't rise to success without having the attitude of a conqueror and that takes faith.

FAITH WITHOUT CORRESPONDING ACTION IS DEAD

As I stated before, there is a renewing of the mind that one has to go through in learning another language. Consequently, shortly after arriving in Guatemala, I began to do several things in response to that. The Lord instructed me to listen to Spanish radio and broadcasts of T. L. Osborn's[10] Mexican crusade messages that had been translated into Spanish. For many hours a day over a period of several weeks, listened to these messages.

It was not always easy. I had many tough days where my mind felt as though it was going to explode. I can remember my head pounding with pain after listening to the radio for several hours, sometimes only understanding one out of every 10 words. It was a daunting task, but I stayed with it and forced myself to continue listening, knowing I was acclimating my mind to the Spanish language. Day after day, week after week, I slowly programmed my mind to hear and then understand the Spanish language.

It was my faith put in action.

WHATEVER IT TAKES!

The Bible says in Romans 10:17 that faith comes by hearing and hearing by the Word. And I say, "So does learning another language!" It starts with hearing, then understanding...and then speaking brings results.

I lived with a small dictionary in my back pocket, which I still have. Many of my early conversations were very laborious. It often took 10 to 15 minutes just to say simple sentences, but I stayed with it.

Whether you are learning a second language or doing anything else in life, there's a powerful lesson to be learned in being consistent and having perseverance. Sticking to something and not quitting is the key to overcoming so many of life's challenges. If we would stick to that diet or exercise program, or that job when work becomes challenging and stressful, or whatever the commitment might be—we would be better off in the long run. It's not a matter of *wanting* something; it's a matter of wanting something enough to stick to it to the end. After all, we all want more fulfilling relationships, more money, and better jobs. The "want" has nothing to do with what we create. It's the tenacity behind the "want" that enables it to come to full manifestation.

In the book written by Brian Klemmer called, *If How-to's Were Enough, We Would All Be Skinny, Rich and Happy*, he talks about this process of wanting to go somewhere or have something by having an attitude of "I'm going to make this happen."[2] It's the "do whatever it takes" attitude in life that brings rewards, fulfillment, and blessings. If you do what you don't want to do, you will become what you want to be.

Faith works the same way. It starts with an absolute assurance based on a fact. Then, the corresponding action creates movement, excitement, and an atmosphere where God can work on your behalf.

CHAPTER SIX

KEY PRINCIPLES

1. We don't have as much a knowing problem as we do a believing problem.

2. People don't rise to success without having the attitude of a conqueror—and that takes faith.

3. Great faith is not moved by your past, age, lack of education, or what people might say.

4. Start with hearing, then understanding. Then, the speaking will brings results.

FIGHT THE FEAR

W hen I was first learning Spanish, I would meet someone and exchange the normal greeting such as:

"¡Hola! ¿Como estas?" (Hi! How are you?)

"Mi nombre es Timoteo," (My name is Tim.)

"¿De donde eres?" (Where are you from?)

Conversations started out pleasantly and in a friendly manner—that is until the Spanish speaker took off talking a 100 miles an hour!

To be polite, I would look them in the eyes and nod, from time to time saying, "¿De veras?" (Really?), which I learned was the best way to keep a conversation going. The problem was I didn't know what they were saying! But as they kept talking, I kept smiling and saying, "¿De veras?" ("Really?")

Eventually, the train derailed when the person stopped sharing the most intimate details of his or her life and asked me a question. Since I didn't know what they were saying, I didn't know what an appropriate answer would be. I *really* felt like a dumb gringo!

When they realized I was completely lost, they would, then, ask that proverbial question: "¿Hablas Español?" (Do you speak Spanish?)

The spirit of fear would then grip me from the top of my head to the soles of my feet. I'd think to myself, "Lord, what do I do now?"

The fear of communicating in Spanish gripped me. I didn't know what to say or how to respond to their question, so I automatically answered, "No hablo Español." (I do not speak Spanish.) In my mind, I thought that was the correct response, and actually, it was the only response.

Afterward, I often became depressed because I couldn't communicate with people in Spanish. I was constantly bombarded with thoughts like, "It's too difficult to learn another language! Just forget it!"

Fear is a powerful force that hinders many people from learning another language. But fear has no place in the life of the believer. You must be aware that you will make mistakes when speaking Spanish. I have, and I'm sure as I continue to grow in my fluency in Spanish, I will make more.

Fear is a tremendous force that hinders so many from learning another language.

Let me teach you a new Spanish word that will help you eliminate fear altogether: "*¡Superalo!*" (pronounced: soop air a low). It means: "Get over it!"

Everyone makes mistakes. So what? *¡Superalo!* No one speaks perfect Spanish, just as no one speaks perfect English. So if you make a mistake, just get over it. No big deal! Refuse to allow fear to hold you back from speaking a foreign language. Actually, *speaking* a language is the fastest and most effective way to learn it.

The Lord helped me get over fear by using humor. One of the greatest tools we have for destroying fear is learning to laugh at ourselves.

Read here what James says:

"Dear brothers, is your life full of difficulties and temptations? Then be happy, for when the way is rough, your patience has a chance to grow."

James 1:2-3 (TLB)

L.O.L.— "LAUGH OUT LOUD"

This is a true story. Several years ago, I was teaching a home Bible study and mostly women were present. I was teaching from Mark 11:23, which says:

"For verily I say unto you, That whosoever shall say unto this mountain, Be thou removed, and be thou cast into the sea; and shall not doubt in his heart, but shall believe that those things which he saith shall come to pass; he shall have whatsoever he saith."

◄ ▪▪▪▪▪▪ ■ ▪▪▪▪▪▪ ►

One of the greatest tools we have for destroying fear is learning to laugh at ourselves.

◄ ▪▪▪▪▪▪ ■ ▪▪▪▪▪▪ ►

I explained what it means in the Bible when the word "whosoever" is used. I then told the group we should make a bold confession of who we are and proceeded to lead the group in a confession.

In Spanish, I instructed the group to repeat after me. I began, "Yo soy." ("I am.") Everyone echoed, "Yo soy. . . ." ("I am.") Then I continued the confession by saying, "Una cualquiera!" ("A whosoever,")...but no one repeated the last phrase. I thought they must not have understood my Spanish, so I proceeded to repeat the exercise by saying again,

"Yo soy." Everyone repeated, "Yo soy." "Una cualquiera." Again, nothing. Silence.

For a third time, I asked the group to please repeat this bold declaration of faith by repeating after me: "Yo soy." They all said, "Yo soy." "Una cualquiera!"

Again, an awkward silence filled the room.

I could not figure out why they sat there completely unresponsive with blank, perplexed looks on their faces!

Finally, a friend of mine leaned over—almost doubling over with pain from laughing—and told me that I was telling them to say, "I am a whore!"

In the context in which I was trying to use the phrase "I am a whosoever," in Spanish the correct way to say it would've been: "Yo soy una persona cualquiera." A small difference in use, but a *huge* difference in meaning!

Although this happened several years ago, we still

laugh about it today!

I tell that story because it was an honest mistake—and an embarrassing one at my expense.

When you make honest mistakes—and you will—learn to laugh at yourself. Afterward, the situation makes for great stories. When you laugh at yourself, you are actually taking authority over fear, and it will not have any place in your life.

THE COMPANION OF FEAR

Pride is a companion to fear. I have found that most people are very gracious when they find out you are learning to speak their language. The Mexican people are some of the most gracious people I have ever met.

What has helped me tremendously is giving people the right to speak into my life. Although some people will openly correct your Spanish, most won't voluntarily tell you when you make a mistake, unless you ask them to. I tell people up front (those that I have a relation-ship with and trust), "Please feel free to tell me if I make an error in my Spanish."

Why do I do this?

Simple.

I want to turn every mistake into a learning experi-ence. By being aware of my mistakes when I make them, I can then learn how to correct them.

Doing this exercise completely killed any pride I might have had left. It helped me keep a humble heart and stay teachable.

Even to this day, after I teach, I have people pass me notes if I have made a conjugational error. I keep those notes, write them down, and store them in a file. From time to time, I go back and review them.

Pride has no place in learning a new language.

When fear and pride are working together, they form a powerful force that only hinders people from learning another language. Sometimes I think God wants to see what it takes to make us quit. The question is: are we going to bow down to fear, or are we going to stand up to this bully in the name of Jesus? Are we going to allow pride to stunt our growth?

◀ ▥▥▥ ■ ▥▥▥ ▶

Faith takes risks. Faith has no fear.

◀ ▥▥▥ ■ ▥▥▥ ▶

It takes faith to learn another language because it takes faith to come against fear and pride.

> *"...God has not given us a spirit of fear, but of power and of love and of a sound mind."*
>
> ### 2 Timothy 1:7 (NKJV)

We must take our authority over fear and pride to move on to the next level. They have no place in the realm of faith.

THROUGH THE EYES OF A CHILD

Children can learn to speak another language much quicker than adults because they are fearless. Our children were two, four, and five years of age when we first arrived in Mexico. In less than six months, they became fluent in Spanish.

"Why?" you ask.

I asked myself that same question. Then I began to notice some things. As I watched them playing with other children, I noticed they had an uncanny way of communicating. Each child would speak in their own native language, even though I knew they could not understand each other's words. However, the children seemed to be communicating through body language, tones, and gestures. I noticed they had no fear of expressing their desires or wants with each other and

◄IIIIIIII ■ IIIIIIII►

When fear and pride are working together, they form a powerful force that only hinders people from learning another language.

◄IIIIIIII ■ IIIIIIII►

definitely had no pride.

After a few weeks, Hannah (our oldest daughter), began to learn a few words. She didn't know how to conjugate Spanish verbs or how to correctly pronounce certain words, but she just went for it. No fear!

At first, she would mix some Spanish and English together in her sentences. Even though it was not grammatically correct, she was communicating. Then she would teach her younger sister, Tiffany, and then her brother, Matthew. She was only five years old, but in less than six months, she was fluent in Spanish and speaking with a perfect Spanish accent.

In May of 2009, Hannah graduated from high school, having completed all of her formal elementary and secondary education on the mission field in Mexico City. She is fully bi-lingual, as are her two younger siblings.

Children have no inhibitions or fear of how they may sound, nor do they care how well they conjugate verbs. We can learn so much from them. If we are going to learn a new language, we need to put aside our inhibitions and begin to communicate just like they do. Good accent, bad accent, good grammar, bad grammar—children make it happen.

JUST GO FOR IT!

As adults, we have to get beyond the fear of what others might think about us. We can become too consumed with our image. What we need to do is to take a chance!

That's right! Go for it! Start a conversation with someone by asking them something about themselves, and perhaps you'll find yourself in the middle of a great time exchanging thoughts and ideas in a new language.

Have faith in people. Most people are understanding and gracious when they hear someone learning to speak a new language. Learn to overcome your fears and inhibitions in communicating with others. Faith takes risks. Faith has no fear. If you are going to conquer your fears and inhibitions, you have to take the Nike® challenge and "Just Do It."™

Imagine this. Where would we be if some of the people we have learned from had been hindered by their fear of what others thought?

"SORRY, I DON'T DO...."

There's a story about an employee who was griping about his new job at a seminary. He thought he was too qualified for the type of work that was assigned to him. The seminary professor overheard another employee telling the one complaining, "Look, the world is a better place because Michael Angelo didn't say, 'I don't do ceilings.' "

If you ask me, I think the world is a better place because the Wright brothers didn't say, "We don't do heights;" and Martin Luther King Jr. didn't say, "I don't do speeches;" and Daniel didn't say, "I don't do lions' dens;" and David didn't say, "I don't do giants;" and the apostle Paul didn't say, "I don't do correspondence;" and Jesus *never* said, "I don't do crosses."

Think about it. The world will be a better place when you overcome your fear of what others might think.

CHAPTER SEVEN

KEY PRINCIPLES

---

1. Learn to laugh at your mistakes.

2. Follow the example of a child—make it happen!

3. Faith takes risks.

4. No fear.

5. Deal with fear and pride by humbling yourself and allowing others to speak into your life by correcting your Spanish.

6. Stay teachable by keeping notes when you learn something new. Keep those notes in a file and review them from time to time.

7. Just do it!™

THE POWER OF COMMUNICATION

We connect with people through words, and words are powerful. By giving a heart-felt compliment or an encouraging word to inspire someone else, you may cause that person to open up to you and help you learn. The very person you may be reaching out to can give *you* something valuable in return and help you advance to the next level of learning.

YOU ARE A SPEAKING SPIRIT

Several years ago, my wife and I attended a conference in Hawaii. One of the speakers was Jesse Duplantis, who taught a message that people are speaking spirits.[1] And since that time, that phrase has stuck with me.

Mankind is created in the image and likeness of God. We were created by God; and as His children, we are to act like Him.

Jesus said in John 4:24, "*God is a spirit. . . .*" Since God created man in His image, man is also a spirit. (See Genesis 1:26.) I like to say it like this, "I am a spirit, I have a soul, and I live in an earthly body."

In Genesis chapter one, the wonderful story of creation is recorded. What is so interesting about how God created the heavens and the earth is just that: *how* He did it.

Each time Scripture says, "God said," it then continues, "and it was so." God creates with His words. He is a faith God, and faith is primarily released though the words we speak. Look at this verse of scripture and think about the new birth:

"That if you confess with your mouth, 'Jesus is Lord', and believe in your heart that God raised him from the dead, you will be saved. For it is with your heart that you believe and

are justified, and it is <u>with your mouth</u> that you <u>confess</u> and are saved."

Romans 10:9-10 (NIV)

Our lives are comprised of the things we have said. Everything we have today is a result of what we said yesterday. Words are powerful tools that can keep us from attaining our life's goals or enable us to fulfill them. People who are raised in a negative environment and are constantly talking about what they do not have and what they cannot do, usually accomplish just that—nothing.

◀ ▌▌▌▌▌▌ ■ ▌▌▌▌▌▌ ▶

Everything we have today is a result of what we said yesterday.

◀ ▌▌▌▌▌▌ ■ ▌▌▌▌▌▌ ▶

God has given us a very powerful tool: our ability to communicate and create through words. That's why I like to say that I am a speaking spirit. God created us to use our words to set a direction for our lives and allow us to bless others. Speaking faith-filled words and confessing God's Word in our lives gives Him a platform to work *in* us and *through* us.

Speaking truth and life into others is our God-given gift. It's a spiritual exercise that creates hope and helps people reach their maximum potential in Christ. Make a commitment today to be a person of hope, a carrier or messenger of truth with powerful words to deposit into the lives of others. We are *speaking spirits* who can change our world through our words.

Start in your own vernacular—your own language—and then use the principles in this book to supernaturally learn another language and double your opportunities to create hope and healing in people's lives through your words.

DON'T NEGATE YOUR FAITH WITH YOUR WORDS

Now here is something else the Lord taught me. Don't ever say you don't speak the language you are learning. As I said in Chapter Seven, in the beginning, I was fearful of not having the words to answer a question and would answer, "No, hablo Español." ("I don't speak Spanish.") However, the Lord corrected me and instructed me never to speak that over myself.

You see, faith is released primarily through words.

If you want to learn to speak another language *supernaturally,* you need to understand how faith works. It starts by believing in your heart that you can, and then expressing that belief with words. You would not say, "I am *not* going to the dentist today," and then *go*. Instead, you would make an appointment, record the date, plan your day, tell your boss that you have a dentist appointment, and *then* go.

The reason the Lord told me not to say, "I don't speak Spanish," was because my words were negating my faith. How silly to say you don't speak something that you are attempting to speak. Instead of saying, "I don't speak Spanish," He told me to say, "Estoy aprendiendo hablar Español." ("I am learning to speak Spanish.")

Stay positive in your faith's confession when learning a language. If someone asks you a question and you don't know the answer, just say, "I don't know," or "No se." Don't negate your faith by saying that you don't speak the language you desire to speak. Let those who want to learn another language say, "*I am learning to speak!*"

"Let the weak say, 'I am strong!' "

Joel 3:10b

GET A PLAN AND WORK THE PLAN

I am convinced that there is a lot more power and potential in our words than we really know. Words create or destroy; they lift up or pull down. They need to be understood so they produce the results we need in this world. Look at what the book of Proverbs has to say about the power of our words:

"The tongue has the power of life and death and those who love it will eat its fruit."

Proverbs 18:21 (NIV)

Take a moment and analyze your speech. What kind of words do you use to express yourself to others? Are they uplifting, encouraging, and positive, or do you have a tendency to be self-deprecating, cynical, or negative? How do you talk about situations, others, your family, and your personal life? I would encourage you to take an inventory of what you say.

One of the main functions of a corporation's CEOs is to solve problems within the corporation. However, before they can solve a problem, they must be able to recognize a problem. Those CEOs who are unable to identify problems within their organization, prioritize them, and then develop a plan of action to resolve those problems, are more than likely going to be fired. The bottom line: in order to succeed, they have to have a plan. My wife likes to say it this way: "Get a plan and work the plan."

Here is a simple plan you can follow to examine your words, and at the same time, eliminate any pride. Have a good friend, a spouse, or a co-worker take inventory of your words. This person needs to be someone you trust and who will be completely truthful with you.

By "inventory" I mean, at the end of a conversation or at the end of the day, ask that person for an honest evaluation of your words. On a scale of one to ten—with "one" being the most negative and "ten" being the most positive—how did you do? Were you mostly positive when talking about your current situation, your boss, your kids, your finances, or other topics of conversation?

◄ ▪▪▪▪▪▪▪▪▪ ■ ▪▪▪▪▪▪▪▪ ►

Not only is God a God of order, but He is also a God who loves individuality.

◄ ▪▪▪▪▪▪▪▪▪ ■ ▪▪▪▪▪▪▪▪ ►

If you scored a six, ask yourself what it would take to be a seven...and so on. Re-evaluate your progress, continue working on your plan, and soon you will start moving toward being a positive and encouraging individual whom people will love to be around.

VOICE OF DISTINCTION

God is so awesome in that He has created each and every one of us with our own distinct qualities, each with our own DNA. With more than six billion people on this earth, no two have the same finger prints, voice distinction, or gifts. Being unique is part of God's master plan, as each and every one of us has been created to complete something that no other person can. *You* are *UNFORGETTABLE!*

Think about our universe and how unique God's creation is. Scientists are fascinated with it and long to find out its origin and how it all works together.

...give voice to your gift.

In the city of Copenhagen, Holland, you will find an astronomical clock. It is one the most complicated clocks in the world. It took locksmith Jens Olsen 40 years to plan and mathematically compute the movement of the gear mechanisms for the clock and it cost more than one million dollars to build. The clock has 10 faces and 15,000 pieces. It keeps the time in weeks, months, and years, as well as calculates the movement of the planets. Some of its pieces will not move for 25 centuries. What is so interesting about this clock is that it loses only three seconds every 1,000 years.[2] As with all clocks, this intricate time piece is regulated by a "clock" that is more precise and more accurate—the universe. The universe is a clock with millions of stars and pieces moving century after century so precisely that all time on earth is measured by it.

Not only is God a God of order, He is also a God who loves individuality. What a unique and precise world we live in. If God made the universe so precise and unique, consider the precision He used to create His own children, each one *unique* in gifts, talents, and abilities.

◄ ▉▉▉▉▉ ▪ ▉▉▉▉▉ ►

The unique voice—the lingo—you have in this world was given to you for a powerful purpose.

◄ ▉▉▉▉▉ ▪ ▉▉▉▉▉ ►

The unique voice—the lingo—you have in this world was given to you for a powerful purpose. *Lingo* means "the language and speech, jargon, and slang of a particular group or individual." We all have our own way of communicating, sharing, and expressing feelings. We also have a unique message or truth that God wants us to deposit in others, something *they* need to encourage them to go to the next level.

I like something a friend of mine, Dr. Dean Radtke says: "God brings people to our side because there is something in us He wants to deposit in them, so that in 20 years from now, they can go 10 time zones one way and six blocks another way to start a work or touch a life."[3]

Think about how God used someone in your life to encourage you. Then at a later time, you were able to use that same truth or encouraging word to help someone else through a difficult time or help someone make a good decision.

Most people know the difference between flattery and genuine heart-felt support. Empty, superficial words might fill a temporary self-centered need; but in the long run, they won't pay any dividends. On the other hand, faith-filled words build, encourage, instill hope, and provide assurance. Their deposits yield great reward. So give voice to your gift.

CHAPTER EIGHT

KEY PRINCIPLES

1. You are a speaking spirit.

2. Everything you have today is a result of what you said yesterday.

3. Words are powerful tools that can keep you from attaining your life's goals or allow you to fulfill them.

4. You are a carrier of hope.

5. God created each and every one of us unique in gifts, talents, and abilities.

6. Instead of saying you don't speak the language, say, "Estoy aprendiendo hablar Español," ("I am learning to speak Spanish.")—or whatever language you are learning to speak.

7. You have a unique voice print; use it to bless others.

DIVINE CONNECTIONS

God puts people in your path for a purpose. These relationships should be valued at every level. These divine connections are designed to be a blessing and encouragement in your life's journey.

Paul talked about divine relationship and said it like this:

"I planted, Apollos watered, but God [all the while] was making it grow and [He] gave the increase."

1 Corinthians 3:6 (AMP)

I think it's important to note that God makes use

of a variety of instruments and fits them to their uses and intentions. Paul was fitted for the planting work, while Apollos was fitted for the watering work.

Whether we do the planting or the watering, God is going to be glorified because others are better off and more equipped for their purpose in life.

EVERYONE NEEDS A PÉPE

When I lived in Guatemala, an elderly man named Pépe worked in front of the house I lived in. Pépe was in charge of keeping the records of the city buses that passed in front of this house. I spent untold hours talking with Pépe. He would help me with my car if I needed to change the oil, wash it, or give it a tune up.

Pépe didn't care how little Spanish I spoke or how difficult it was for me at first to express even the smallest detail. He was a kind, well-spoken gentleman doing his job and helping a young 20 year-old learn a new language.

Pépe didn't have all his teeth. He didn't have more

than a fifth-grade education, and he didn't make more than $40 a month. But for me, Pépe was a gem of a man, and I will never forget him. God brought Pépe across my path to help me touch thousands of souls for the Kingdom of God.

Pépe didn't speak a word of English, and yet we talked for hours. We talked about the weather, the country, his work, and his family. Whatever was happening in the world, we talked about it—almost always with my dictionary in hand just in case I came across a word I didn't know. We had great fellowship, and he became a great friend.

God brought Pépe across my path to help me touch thousands of souls for the Kingdom.

Learning a language does take time, but I think one of the best tools is finding a divine connection—a "Pépe"—someone who does not speak English, so you are forced to *think* and *speak in their language*. I knew very few English-speaking people in Guatemala at that time, and I thought, *If I don't speak the language, I won't eat!* Sometimes hunger can be a pretty good motivator!

CHAPTER NINE

KEY PRINCIPLES

1. God puts people in your path for a purpose. These relationships should be valued at every level.

2. Remember, whether you do the planting or the watering, God is going to be glorified because others are better off and more equipped for their purpose in life.

3. One of the best tools in learning a language is finding a divine connection—a "Pépe"—someone who does not speak English, so that you are forced to *think* and *speak in his or her language*.

THE LEARNING CURVE

I n this chapter, you will learn some powerful keys the Lord taught me in understanding the process involved in learning to speak a new language. As with most language learning programs, there is a learning curve and there are cause-and-effect results. The effort you put forward and the time you invest will determine the outcome of your learning.

TOTAL EMERSION

I believe that living in the country where the language you desire to learn is the main spoken language is, by far, the quickest and most effective way to learn a new language.

There are many advantages to what I call "total immersion." Total immersion is not only learning the language, but also learning the culture surrounding the language and the context in which things are said and phrases are used.

If you desire to learn Spanish but cannot live in a Spanish-speaking country, then I suggest finding an authentic Mexican restaurant in your town where all the cooks and waiters only speak Spanish. Take the time to get to know them and become interested in their lives, their occupation, and their hobbies. Establish a rapport by finding something you have in common with them, such as favorite foods, surroundings, sports, history, or life experiences. Find out their names and begin developing a relationship with them. Visit their churches, bazaars, parties, and gatherings where everyone is speaking Spanish. Try to immerse yourself in their culture as much as possible. It is a great way to meet people, build relationships, and learn a new language.

Get out of your comfort zone and remember that your ultimate purpose is to invest in others. A conversation might start out quite elementary; but if your purpose is to deposit something valuable into someone's life, it will not go unrewarded. Look for a way to compliment them; and most importantly, give value first. As I said earlier, make sure you are sincere. It's easy to detect someone who complements others but does not have any sincerity in his or her words.

THE UPS PACKAGE FACTOR

I found that when learning a new language, knowledge comes in what I call "information packages." If you've ever ordered something over the Internet or through a catalog and had it shipped by UPS®, your order may arrive in different packages if it is a large order. And most likely, those packages will not arrive at the same time. In the same way, learning occurs in stages. And just like you don't always receive all of your packages at the same time, you don't learn everything you need to know at one time.

◄ ▮▮▮▮▮▮▮ ▪ ▮▮▮▮▮▮▮ ►

Learning a new language can be a thrill, not a thriller!

◄ ▮▮▮▮▮▮▮ ▪ ▮▮▮▮▮▮▮ ►

You'll find that as you continue to study and learn, someone will show you or teach you something valuable that will "click" on the inside of you. All of a sudden, you have that *"Ah, ha! I get it!"* experience. And this is part of the learning process.

As I mentioned in an earlier chapter, your everyday connections with people are vital to your learning process.

◄ ▊▊▊▊▊▊ ■ ▊▊▊▊▊▊ ►

We can eliminate the frustration of learning a new language by simply committing to our purpose of adding value to others.

◄ ▊▊▊▊▊▊ ■ ▊▊▊▊▊▊ ►

Every time you meet someone who speaks the Spanish language—or whatever language you are learning—you should view that meeting as an opportunity to receive the "special package" they have for you that contains information to help your learning experience. It may be some little tidbit, such as the way they pronounce a certain word, conjugate a verb, or construct a sentence. Regardless of how minute it may seem, when you receive one of these information packages, write down what you have learned, so you can review it at a later time.

LEARNING FROM THE NATIONALS

Another thing the Lord taught me was the value of learning from the nationals. I would have Americans teach me something in Spanish, only to find out months later that I had learned to say it incorrectly. Listening to the pronunciation of Americans only confused me, so I made it a point to learn from those who speak in the native tongue. Now, don't get me wrong. There are Americans I know who were born and raised in Mexico who speak Spanish fluently with no American accent.

However, when I lived in Guatemala, I didn't know anyone like that, so I learned accents and pronunciation only from the nationals. It made all the difference in the world in my learning process.

In Guatemala, we had lots of helpers around the house and office. When the maids were cooking, I would love to get right in there and help, ask questions, and talk to them. It wasn't customary for a foreigner to converse with the hired help but I didn't care. It was a great learning opportunity for me and gave me a platform to put into practice what I had learned without any fear or reservation.

PHRASEOLOGY

Most language schools give you books filled with nouns and verbs. The mind-blowing number of nouns and the dozens of ways to conjugate every verb can be overwhelming, to say the least.

The Lord taught me something I refer to as "phraseology." Instead of memorizing thousands of nouns, He told me to learn Spanish phrases. For example, I would learn how to say phrases such as:

"¿Donde esta el _____?"

(Where is the _____?)

"¿Me puedes decir como pronunciar _____?"

(Can you tell me how to pronounce _____?)

"¿Como se dice _____?"

(How do you say _____?)

Then I would fill in the blank with any suitable noun.

◄ ▐▐▐▐▐▐ ■ ▐▐▐▐▐▐ ►

I looked for every opportunity to practice what I had learned every day, looking for new ways to use each new word or phrase in a sentence. Then I would write it down and later rehearse it with a friend.

Instead of memorizing thousands of nouns, He told me to learn Spanish phrases.

The most effective way to learn is to teach what you know. By putting into practice little phrases and words, I was not only storing up information in my head, but also allowing it to get into my heart and soul. It was becoming a part of

◄ ▐▐▐▐▐▐ ■ ▐▐▐▐▐▐ ►

◄ ▐▐▐▐▐▐ ■ ▐▐▐▐▐▐ ►

The most effective way to learn is to teach what you know.

◄ ▐▐▐▐▐▐ ■ ▐▐▐▐▐▐ ►

me—my second nature, if you will. I was renewing my mind with Spanish.

Not only did I learn how to say a phrase correctly, but I could carry on conversations with ease. Later, I learned more complicated phrases that required tense changes.

Start with the simple phrases, and in time as you continue putting into practice the principles taught in this book, the more difficult phrases will come. Until then, ask questions, take notes, give people permission to correct you, and use what you have learned by putting it into daily practice.

KEEP THE JOY IN LEARNING

I encourage you to start learning a new language by immersing yourself in the culture and by practicing phraseology. Doing these things will get you started down the right track in learning another language.

You will find that when your conversation is guided by these basic steps, learning a new language can be a thrill, not a thriller! Whatever you do, *MAKE IT FUN!* If it's not fun, it's not going to be easy.

We can eliminate the frustration of learning a new language by simply committing to adding value to others. Give what you have and great opportunities will open up to you.

CHAPTER TEN

KEY PRINCIPLES

---

1. Immerse yourself in the language you are learning.

2. Discover the information package in everyone.

3. Your ultimate purpose is to invest in others.

4. Learn in phrases.

5. If it's not fun, it's not going to be easy.

FOLLOW YOUR GIFT

Shortly after arriving in Guatemala, I knew exactly what I wanted to do. I had a burning desire to teach in the training center. After all, that is what my gift is. It's what I live for. However, as much as I love to teach, I have never liked using an interpreter. I don't have anything against interpreters; it's simply a personal preference. I've always felt that waiting for an echo was more of an *interrupter* than an *interpreter*. I prefer having that one-on-one opportunity to teach people. It's more personal, and there's a better flow of receiving the Word and ministry without any breakdown in communication. And it's easier to minister to people's hearts, which is the most important thing of all. Because of that, I had a lot of motivation to learn the Spanish language quickly.

Learning a language was a means to an end. It was simply what I needed to do to express my gift. I could hardly wait to teach. Then about two months after arriving in Guatemala, I was given my first opportunity. I was asked to teach a class in the Bible school—in Spanish!

If you had heard me teach that first time in Quetzaltenango, Guatemala, you probably would not have been as excited as I was. My Spanish was very awkward, slow, and even "gringo-ish," but I was in heaven! I was living my dream, and teaching in Spanish without an interpreter. I was having the time of my life and operating in my anointing.

For the next two years, I continued to grow in my knowledge of the language, speaking Spanish every day. Amazingly, I began translating for the missionary I came to work for. Some people got upset with me for learning the language so quickly. But I kept a humble heart and continued to do what I loved to do, which is teach.

EXPRESSING YOUR GIFT

Language helps you express your gift, which is designed to help others and add value to their lives. Your voice also gives God a voice in the world. By learning another language, you are giving God even more opportunities to touch lives.

Everyone has their reasons for needing or desiring to learn a second language. You may be a public speaker, school teacher, or a businessman. For me, I needed to learn Spanish to better express the gift God had given me. Whatever your profession or role in life is, learning another language will open more doors to better express your gift to more people.

God gives ability to fulfill responsibility. That's your assignment... your gift.

Don't limit yourself to only one level of expression. Challenge yourself to get out of your comfort zone and learn a new language. Break through the language barrier. And as you do, you will double your effectiveness on this earth for the Kingdom of God.

If you're a writer and already have material in English, take an extra step of faith and have that material translated into another language—one you have in your heart. God honors faith; and as you take that step, I believe the resources and finances will come.

Remember, *you* are responsible to stir up *your* gift and give it freedom of expression. God gives ability to fulfill responsibility. That's your assignment—your gifting.

CHAPTER ELEVEN

KEY PRINCIPLES

1. Your voice gives God a voice in the world.

2. Learning another language gives God more opportunity to touch more lives.

3. Speaking another language opens more doors to better express your gift to more people.

4. You are responsible to stir up the gift within you.

THE SEASON
OF PREPARATION

After two wonderful years in Guatemala, I felt in my heart it was time to go back to Broken Arrow, Oklahoma. During my stay in Guatemala, RHEMA had transitioned from being a one-year Bible school to a two-year Bible school and training center.

I knew in my heart that I needed to return to school to finish my ministerial training. It wasn't easy, but I felt it was the right thing to do.

My heart was torn in leaving Guatemala, but somehow I knew I would be back in a Spanish-speaking nation one day. Little did I know then that I would never live in Guatemala again. I have visited the country on several occasions and that nation and the people are dear to my heart.

As the Lord instructed, I returned to Broken Arrow to finish my training. I had no idea that God had more training in mind for me than a second year of Bible studies. In August of 1984, I began to work for Kenneth Hagin Ministries.[1] What I thought would only be a one or two-year stint, turned into 11 1/2 years of service and training at Kenneth Hagin Ministries.

Although the experience and friendships gained were invaluable, my heart continued to beat for the Hispanic people.

When God gives you a gift, it's for His purposes; and it's there to stay.

It's interesting to see how God unfolds our destiny and His plan for our lives. For each of us, His plan is different; yet, the fulfillment of those plans are the same. He brings them about during different seasons of our lives. General Norman Schwarzkopf, retired four-star general for the U.S. Army, couldn't have said it more perfectly. He said, "Life is like a collection of seasons."[2]

And that was exactly what those 11 1/2 years spent in Broken Arrow, Oklahoma were. My time at Kenneth Hagin Ministries was a season of more preparation.

During that time, I had only a handful of opportunities to teach or speak in Spanish. But it was also during that time that God taught me an invaluable principle: If I was willing to go through the small doors, He would open the big doors.

A DREAM FULFILLED

In January of 1996, my wife and I and our three small children took a giant leap of faith and moved from Tulsa, Oklahoma, to Mexico City, Mexico. God was leading us to start a church and a Bible training center.

By the time we were preparing to leave for Mexico, I had spent nearly 14 years in the U.S. My time in the States was far removed from the language and the culture of the Mexican people, and I had hardly spoken any Spanish during those 14 years.

◄ ▪ ►

...when God gives you a gift, it's for His purposes; and it's there to stay.

◄ ▪ ►

People will tell you that after learning the native tongue of a country, once you leave, you risk losing your fluency in that language. The longer you're away, the greater the chance of losing the language you had learned. Worse, the likelihood of regaining what you once knew becomes quite slim.

So in the natural, it seemed that being away for 14 years would be a tough mountain to climb. But within a month of stepping back onto Mexican soil, we started a home Bible study; and I was teaching in Spanish as though I had never left Guatemala 14 years prior. God is so good!

You see, when God gives you a gift, it's for His purposes; and it's there to stay.

"For God's gifts and His call are irrevocable. [He never withdraws them when once they are given, and He does not change His mind about those to whom He gives His grace or to whom He sends His call."]

Romans 11:29 (AMP)

CHAPTER TWELVE

KEY PRINCIPLES

1. Take each of life's seasons as an opportunity to learn and grow.

2. God will open big doors if you are willing to go through the small doors.

3. God orders our steps; we just have to put on our shoes.

4. Right time...right place...right tools.

THE NEED FOR ACCELERATED MINISTRY

You might be asking yourself, "Why is there a need for accelerated ministry?" The reason is simple. Our world is accelerating at an amazing pace; and while it does, the Church must accelerate with it.

Effectively communicating and learning a second—or a third—language are both vital parts of that acceleration process. For those who know a second or third language, God can use them to maximize their effectiveness in the earth to spread the Gospel to many nations.

KNOWLEDGE AND TECHNOLOGY

Increased knowledge and advanced technology have

both accelerated tremendously in the past 100 years. You and I have witnessed this age of exponential growth first-hand.

For example, look at how the transportation industry alone has changed throughout the centuries, beginning with ground transportation. Around 3500 B.C., the first fixed wheels on a cart were invented, and in 2000 B.C., man first began to use horses with carts.[1] Not until the year 1769, was the first road-worthy vehicle invented.[2] The first car ever powered by steam was invented by Ferdinand Verbiest in the year 1672. Ferdinand, a missionary to China was an experimentalist who built his first car in China, where you could rightly say, "The first car ever was made in China."[3] With over 600 million vehicles in the world today and the current rate at which manufacturers are producing, the number of cars will double in the next 30 years.[4]

Now, let's take a look at air transportation. In 1903, the first airplane was built. Commercial airlines, in the year 2000, carried approximately 1.09 billion people on 18 million flights world-wide. Today, nearly three million people around the world fly on commercial aircrafts every day.[5] Air travel has also become a common part of everyday life.

Just like commercial air travel, space travel has become almost as commonplace. It was only in 1969, that the first man walked on the moon. Today, space shuttles lift off into space on scientific explorations and space station maintenance trips so frequently, it's hard to keep up with them. In years past, when a space shuttle would launch from Kennedy Space Center in Florida, large groups would gather in view of the massive launch pad; and the world would pause to watch their televisions as the shuttle took off into outer space. Now, you hardly ever hear about their launches. What you do hear about is the ability for average, everyday people to now pay money to go up into space.

Years from now, who knows where we'll be?

This past century has seen tremendous change in the landscape of our nation. Until in 1900, the beginning of the 20th century, there were only 144 miles of paved roads in the United States.[6] Until 1900, home birth was the typical birth setting for Americans. More than 94% of people worldwide were born at home and did not have telephones, and most did not graduate from high school.[7] More than 86% of Americans did not even own a bathtub, and many had no reliable access to electricity.[8]

Consider how much technology-driven change has compounded over the past century, and imagine an equivalent or greater amount of progress occurring in the generation to come.

Over the past 30 to 35 years, there has been a tremendous increase in micro-computers which has enabled our society to have spectacular progress. They are saying that the power and speed of computers doubles nearly every 18 months. With the increase of cellular phones and cheap computers, the wealth of knowledge from the Internet now is reaching into rural areas of developing countries which has major implications for increased distance learning and education.

SATAN'S KINGDOM IS MOVING AT AN ACCELERATED PACE

In addition to the exponential increase of knowledge and technology, never before in history has there been a greater acceleration of evil in the world. It seems as though Satan and his cohorts are working overtime to create more chaos, confusion, strife, hatred, and war. It's as though the devil senses that his time is growing shorter, and he is panicking.

Moral decline and violence are on the rise across the globe. Sickness, disease, and epidemics, such as AIDS, are killing off entire generations of people groups, leaving many children homeless and parentless in many African countries. We have seen the breakdown of the home and the family unit, as divorces increase, especially among Christian believers.[9] For the United States, the past few years have shown incredible financial instability, and we experienced the failure of the American banking system and a nosedive and vulnerability in the major stock markets. And since 9/11, the world has been on alert as more terrorist threats loom in America, as well as in other parts of the world.

NATURAL DISASTER ACCELERATION

Historically, natural disasters have increased in frequency on the earth. In more recent years, the intensity and frequency to which they are occurring has caught the attention of the media worldwide.

Wikipedia lists the top 10 deadliest natural disasters in the history of mankind. The oldest recorded disaster was the Antioch earthquake, which occurred in 526 A.D. It's interesting to note that seven of the top 10 natural disasters occurred within the past 200 years, killing nearly 7.5 million people. Five of the top 10 deadliest earthquakes have occurred since 1920, and four of those within the past 40 years.[10]

Don't limit yourself to just one level of expression. Challenge yourself to get out of your comfort zone...

A catastrophic natural disaster occurred in January 2010. The 7.0-magnitude earthquake shook the foundations of the city of Port-au-Prince, Haiti. The ground literally opened up and swallowed tall-standing buildings in broad daylight. Many of these buildings were fully occupied with people at their places of employment or attending school. The quake left the small, already-impoverished country devastated and in a massive heap of rubble. Over 200,000 people died.[11] An additional 300,000 people were injured during the initial quake and the strong aftershocks that followed.[12] Of those injured, thousands of amputations were performed in horrific, World War II-like, makeshift triage tents.[13]

The earthquake in Haiti will go down in the history books as one of the worst natural disasters ever known to man.

The deadliest famines worldwide date back to 1315 A.D. Eight of the top 10 have occurred since 1920, killing nearly 100 million people.[14] Still today, every day in third-world countries, thousands suffer from a lack of food and clean drinking water. They lack proper medical care, medical technology, and necessary medications like antibiotics and vaccines to treat their people.

SUPERNATURAL ACCELERATION IS FOR A PURPOSE

Supernatural acceleration is not occurring by chance; it is a sign of the times. The Christian believer, however, has no reason to fear. The acceleration of activity on the earth corresponds precisely with Bible prophecy. It is for a purpose, to fulfill what has been prophesied in the Word of God. Jesus said that Israel was to be our timepiece. (See Matthew 24.) Look closely, watch, and pay attention to what is happening in this tiny nation. For over 2,000 years, it was prophesied that Israel would become a nation; and in 1948, that prophecy was fulfilled. In 1967, the city of Jerusalem was taken back by the Jews. No other nation, or group of dispersed people, has *ever* returned to their homeland to become a nation again.

GOD IS LOOKING FOR A FEW GOOD MEN

It is so important to realize what is happening around us and to understand that God's plan is to do a quick work in the earth today. He needs to move, build, train, and send His workforce out to all four corners of the earth, and He needs to do it at an accelerated pace.

Even the ability to access and acquire knowledge of the Word of God has seen supernatural acceleration. Never before have we had more teaching, books, DVDs, Bible aids, reference materials, conferences, Internet and satellite broadcasts, podcasts, blogs, and e-zines so easily accessible at our fingertips. The Word of God is being preached in an unprecedented way.

Technology, knowledge, and the fulfillment of Bible prophecy are all moving forward at a supernatural pace—all with a purpose. So why would God not want to accelerate the expression of gifts He has instilled in Christians to accomplish His purpose on the earth today? God is looking for highly-skilled and trained believers who know their authority and can look at any challenge and say, like Joshua and Caleb, "Give me that mountain!" (See Numbers 13:27; Numbers 14:6–9; Joshua 14:7–13.)

As you implement the keys in this book for learning a new language, I believe you will multiply your effectiveness for His Kingdom. In Spanish, we use the phrase, "Si, se puede!" or "Yes, you can!"

Remember to make learning another language fun, stay in faith, and never forget that it's for the purpose of depositing a nugget of truth, an encouragement, or a blessing into someone else's life.

CHAPTER THIRTEEN

KEY PRINCIPLES

1. Don't limit yourself to just one level of expression. Challenge yourself to get our of your comfort zone.

2. The signs of the times show us that God wants to do a quick work in the earth today.

3. God is looking for highly-skilled and trained believers who know their authority.

4. Always remember, "Yes, you can!"

THE END TO THE MEANS

My family and I have lived in Mexico for over 14 years. We have served the Mexican community through our church and Bible training center. Working with such wonderful people has brought tremendous joy to our lives. We feel so blessed to have the privilege of having God work in our lives and seeing so many more lives touched through His love and His Word.

Our impact in this nation has been greatly enhanced because of our ability to communicate in Spanish. Sometimes our words may not be perfect; but when they come from the spirit, people open their hearts and appreciate the fact that we are communicating to them in their native language. You don't have to speak perfectly in another language to connect with people. I have heard many people speak in broken English, and I was blessed and encouraged by what they had to say. When it comes from the heart and it's a word in due season, it brings life to your soul.

◄ ▮▮▮▮▮▮ ▪ ▮▮▮▮▮▮ ►

Learning a second language provides you with a powerful tool that allows you to express your gift in a greater way...

◄ ▮▮▮▮▮▮ ▪ ▮▮▮▮▮▮ ►

The S.A.L.E. described in this book is something you can apply to any area of your life, not only to learning a language. It will help you to accomplish your personal goals for your health, your occupation, your education, your finances, your relationships, and every other area of your life.

It all starts with a desire to connect with people and invest in their lives.

THE CONNECTION THAT COUNTS

What's the bottom line? God wants us to move to new

levels of connecting with people, and He wants us to do it quickly. That is the end to the means. And that is what matters. It's making a difference, making an impact in the lives of people.

If you will put into practice the simple principles I have mentioned in this book, I believe you, too, will see supernatural results in learning a new language. You have more God-given potential residing inside of you than you realize. The gifts inside of you were given to you on purpose and for a purpose. As you learn to express those gifts in a greater way, it will leave a lasting and even an eternal impression on others.

Learning a second language provides you with a powerful tool that allows you to express your gift in a greater way and deposit truths in others around the globe. One of my favorite scripture versus says:

> *"Now to Him Who, by (in consequence of) the [action of His] power that is at work within us, is able to [carry out His purpose and] do super-abundantly, far over and above all that we [dare]*

ask or think [infinitely beyond our highest prayers, desires, thoughts, hopes, or dreams]."

Ephesians 3:20 (AMP)

It takes perseverance and a willingness to learn. It involves teaching what we know and giving a voice to our God-given gifts. It takes faith and realizing that we are learning, so as speaking spirits we can impart life-giving words into others.

Make it your prayer today that God will use you beyond anything you could possibly imagine. Be a messenger of hope, depositing truth and life into others.

KEY PRINCIPLES

1. Impact and influence depends on your skill of impartation.

2. Learning a language is born from a desire to connect with someone by speaking to their heart.

3. The bottom line is...connect with people.

4. Be a messenger of hope.

MY PERSONAL TESTIMONY

Tim Rogers Ministries Mexico began in our home with just a handful of people in attendance. In the early years, my wife and I wore many hats: pastors, administrators, worship leaders, ushers, children's workers, and so forth.

At first, it seemed as though we were just a drop in the bucket, trying to reach the more than 25 million people in Mexico City. Since we had not received our legal documentation to operate as a church, I was discouraged because we didn't have a building and had no other way to promote our Bible studies except by word of mouth. I didn't know how we were going to reach more people.

Then one day the Lord helped me. In front of our

home was a metal cage about the size of a large trash can that was used to put our garbage in. Twice a week, the garbage truck would come by and pick up the trash. One day, I noticed a person rummaging through our trash. I watched as he grabbed an old, stale piece of pizza we had thrown away days before. He picked up the pizza, shook off the bugs—or whatever had clung on to it—and began to eat it.

I watched the man eat the pizza like it was the best thing he had eaten in days. I thought to myself, "Man, you've really got to be hungry to go through someone else's trash looking for food."

It was at that moment I heard a voice on the inside of me say, "Yes, and hungry people know where to find the food." All of a sudden, I got it! What the Lord was saying was for me to stay faithful and teach the truths He had taught me, and the hungry people would find me.

We have stayed true to that word. The core of our ministry is solid Bible teaching to help people grow in every area of their lives. We do advertise now; but in those early years, we trusted the Lord to bring people in. And we made sure we provided good spiritual food for the hungry.

As the Bible study grew into a church, the Lord added to our numbers weekly and helpers began to develop! Once we received our legal documentation from the government, we could hold church services in a public auditorium; and we then began holding Sunday services. Several of the initial families who attended our first Bible study are still faithful church members today.

One of the first buildings we rented was an old warehouse we converted into offices and an auditorium. In a few short years, the church grew into two and then three Sunday morning worship services. The need to expand to multiple services became apparent, so we rented the two adjacent buildings to accommodate the people. Today, we rent an even larger facility and in one year's time, we have had to go back to two services, with as many as 1,000 people attending our Sunday services.

We launched RHEMA Bible Training Center Mexico in September 1999 with 24 students. Now we have an average of 100 full-time students each year who come from all over Mexico. About 10 percent of the student body are senior pastors who come to receive biblical training. The hunger in our students to grow in the Word of God is amazing. Many of them travel to school by public transportation four hours one-way to receive the teaching of the Word.

One of our graduates travelled two hours each way to attend school. In his two years of attending the training center, he never missed one day and was never late for class, which is pretty amazing given the culture of "tarde," meaning "late"—which is very acceptable in Mexico.

Along with our regular church services and training center classes, our vision is to reach out to the Mexican people through a variety of mediums. Every year, our ministry hosts many different types of outreaches: evangelistic crusades, medical missions trips, annual men's and women's conferences, and youth conferences. We also work in partnership with many local charitable organizations. God has opened up vast ministry opportunities in the city orphanages and with organizations providing assistance to the thousands of homeless children living on the streets and at the Mexico City dump.

In the past 14 years, we have documented the results of our outreach programs and are blessed to have had the opportunity to reach over 35,000 with the message of salvation followed with water baptisms. In addition to the many saved, we have witnessed thousands healed and hundreds of families having been helped with food and clothing. We have handed out literally thousands of Bibles and have been given permission to go into the locals schools to teach on moral character and basic hygiene.

Other missionaries, evangelists, pastors, teachers, Bible school students, and groups of young people from all over the United States, Canada, and even within the country of Mexico come to visit, support the ministry, minister, and give voice to their gifts as well. We have a thriving church and Bible training center used to disciple people from all over Mexico. God has done some incredible and supernatural things!

Today, I am just as comfortable ministering in Spanish as I am in my mother tongue, English. People are amazed that I don't have a "gringo" (American) accent. I am a living example of how God can supernaturally accelerate you through the learning process of becoming fluent in a second language. To God be the glory!

ENDNOTES

Chapter 1: REALIZATION OF A DREAM

1 RHEMA Bible Training Center opened in 1974 under the direction of Kenneth W. Hagin. In 1976, it moved to its current location in Broken Arrow, Oklahoma, which covers more than 100 acres. I attended RHEMA Bible Training Center for two years, 1979-1980 and 1982-1983.

Chapter 3: MINISTRY BIRTHED FROM DESIRE

1 http://en.wikipedia.org/wiki/French_language_in_Canada

2 www.quoteworld.org/quotes/4458

Chapter 4: LIVING TO GIVE

1 http://www.great-inspirational-quotes.com/zig-ziglar-quotes.html

2 Meyers, Wayne. *Living Beyond the Possible.* Evangeline Press, 2003.

Chapter 5: THE POWER OF PERSEVERANCE

1 Gene Kranz is known to have said this now famous quote, "Failure is not an option," but never did. When the movie *Apollo 13* was being made in 1995, Jerry Bostick, Flight Dynamics Offi-

cer on the Apollo 13, was interviewed by the film writers of
Apollo 13. When asked, "Were there times when people pan-
icked," he   replied, "No, when bad things happened, we just
calmly laid out all the options; and failure was not one of them."
The tag line for the movie came from his reply. http://
www.spaceacts.com/notanoption.htm. Gene Kranz wrote his
book *Failure is Not an Option* in 2000.

2 http://en.wikipedia.org/wiki/Timeline_of_climbing_Mount_
Everest

Chapter 6: THE LANGUAGE OF FAITH

1 T. L. Osborn is a missionary, evangelist, teacher, and author
who has shared the Gospel worldwide to millions of people.
Mexico is one of the 78 nations Mr. Osborn has visited. I had
the privilege of meeting Mr. Osborn in person in 2006 in Seat-
tle, Washington.

2 Klemmer, Brian. *If How-To's Were Enough, We Would All Be
Skinny, Rich, and Happy.* Insight Publishing Group. Sevierville,
Tennessee. 2004.

Chapter 8: THE POWER OF COMMUNICATION

1 Jesse Duplantis, world-renown evangelist, teacher, and speaker
is the founder of Jesse Duplantis Ministries based out of New
Orleans, LA. Jesse Duplantis' television ministry reaches far
beyond the boundaries of the United States.

2 http://www.time.com/time/magazine/article/
0,9171,861920,00.html; http://en.wikipedia.org/wiki/
Jens_Olsen%27s_World_Clock

3 Dr. Dean Radtke is a national and international vision facilitator and strategic planner who equips and positions ministers to become extraordinary leaders. Dr. Radtke ministered at Rhema Mexico in 2005. We continue to benefit from the advice and teaching of Dr. Dean Radtke.

Chapter 12: THE SEASON OF PREPARATION

1 Kenneth Hagin Ministries is a dba for RHEMA Bible Church in Tulsa, OK. I had the privilege of working for this ministry for nearly 12 years in the shipping and receiving department, as well as being the bookstore manager. Reverend Kenneth E. Hagin and Reverend Kenneth Hagin Jr. have authored more than 125 books. More than 58,000 of their teaching tapes are distributed monthly. More information is available at www.rhema.org.

2 Source unknown.

Chapter 13: THE NEED FOR ACCELERATED MINISTRY

1 http://library.thinkquest.org/C004203/science/science02.htm

2 http://listverse.com/2007/09/13/top-10-greatest-inventions/

3 http://www.buzzle.com/articles/who-invented-the-first-ever-car.html

4 "Cars Emit Carbon Dioxide." Global Warming, Focus on the Future, 1997. http://globalwarming.enviroweb.org/ishappening/sources/sources_co2_facts3.html.

5 www.flightattendantcabincrewtraining.com/airlinecrash.htm

6 "America, Start Your Engines." *US News and World Report.* (27 December 1999).

7 http://www.givingbirthnaturally.com/home-birth.html

8 http://jurvetson.blogspot.com/2004/09/accelerating-change-and-societal-shock.html

9 "Born-Again Christian and Divorce: Do They Do Better Than Non-Christian?" Vystas Safroncikas. http://www.truthcast.com/agape/000630christian_divorce. htm. June 30, 2000.

10 http://en.wikipedia.org/wiki/List_of_natural_disasters

11 "Haiti raises earthquake toll to 230,000" *The Washington Post* - February 10, 2010. http://www.washingtonpost.com/wp-dyn/content/article/2010/02/09/AR2010020904447.html.

12 "Haiti will not die, President Rene Preval insists. BBC News. February 12, 2010. http://news.bbc.co.uk/2/hi/americas/8511997.stm.

13 "Amputations become the defining injury of the earthquake in Haiti." Meg Laughlin. St. Petersburg Times. Tampa Bay.com. January 20, 2010. http://www.tampabay.com/news/world/amputations-become-the-defining-injury-of-the-earthquake-in-haiti/1066662.

14 http://en.wikipedia.org/wiki/List_of_natural_disasters#Famines

LET US HEAR FROM YOU...

We, at Tim Rogers Ministries, would love to know what God is doing in your life as a result of you reading this book. Your testimony is a powerful way you can be used to encourage others who are also believing God for supernatural acceleration in their ministry.

We look forward to hearing all the great things God is doing in your life as you begin to apply these principles.

Please take a moment to e-mail us:

usoffice@timrogersministries.org

TIM ROGERS

Tim Rogers is the President of Tim Rogers Ministries, Senior Pastor of Iglesia Biblica RHEMA, and Director of Centro de Entrenamiento Biblico RHEMA of Mexico.

As a missionary statesman with over 27 years of experience in the ministry, Tim's passion is to mentor national leaders in Mexico. Emphasizing faith-based Bible teaching, he is committed to raising the standard of excellence in life and ministry in Mexico. His messages share life-changing truths that faith is the victory and the Word of God never fails!

Tim ministers from the heart of someone who lives what he believes. His first missions experience at the age of 19 changed the course of his life; while on a short-term mission trip to Mexico, the Lord clearly confirmed to him that missions was his calling. One year later, while on a two year term in Guatemala, the Lord supernaturally imparted to him the ability to speak and read the Word of God in Spanish, even though he had not yet received any formal instruction or training. In pursuing God's call to missions, Tim has experienced God's powerful anointing for many dramatic breakthroughs. Over the years, his ministry has taken him to various nations such as Peru, Spain, Columbia, Germany and Panama.

Following his graduation from RHEMA Bible Training

Center in 1983, Tim joined the staff of Kenneth Hagin Ministries. Over the next 12 years, he served as an instructor at the training center, led student mission trips, and taught a School of the Bible class for the church. In January 1996, Tim and his family moved to Mexico to pioneer a church and launch a Bible training center.

Tim and his wife, Rhonda, reside in Mexico City with their three children, Hannah, Tiffany, and Matthew. Together, they are committed to spreading the Gospel in Mexico through the preaching and teaching of the uncompromised Word of God.

CONTACT

In the U.S., write:
Tim Rogers Ministries
P.O. Box 572
Broken Arrow, OK
U.S.A.
74013-0572
1-918-259-4949

In Canada, write:
Tim Rogers Ministries
1930-155th St.
Surrey, B.C.
Canada
V4A 7M9
1-604-536-6605

In Mexico, write:
Tim Rogers Ministries
APDO 416
Av. Pacifico No. 296 Rosedal
Coyoacan, C.P. 04331
Mexico, D.F.
Mexico

Visit us online at:

www.timrogersministries.org
www.rhemamexico.org

**Find us on
Facebook:**